SUMMARY

Never Split The Difference

Chris Voss & Tahl Raz!

Negotiating As If
Your Life Depended On It

FastDigest-Summary

© Copyright 2018 - Present.
All rights reserved.

This document is geared towards providing reliable information in regards to the topic and issue covered. The publication is sold with the idea that the publisher is not required to render accounting, officially permitted, or otherwise, qualified services. If advice is necessary, legal or professional, a practiced individual in the profession shall be ordered.

- From a Declaration of Principles which was accepted and approved equally by a Committee of the American Bar Association and a Committee of Publishers and Associations.

In no way is it legal to reproduce, duplicate, or transmit any part of this document in either electronic means or in printed format. Recording of this publication is strictly prohibited and any storage of this document is not allowed unless with written permission from the publisher. All rights reserved.

The information provided herein is stated to be truthful and consistent, in that any liability, in terms of inattention or otherwise, by any usage or abuse of any policies, processes, or directions contained within is solely and completely the responsibility of the recipient reader. Under no circumstances will any legal responsibility or blame be held against the publisher for any reparation, damages, or monetary loss due to the information herein, either directly or indirectly.

Respective authors own all copyrights not held by the publisher.

TABLE OF CONTENTS

INTRODUCTION 5

SUMMARY 7

  PART 1 – CONTROLLING THE EMOTIONS 7

  PART 2 – ACTIVE LISTENING IS THE KEY 9

  PART 3– PRACTICE EMPATHY......................11

  PART 4: – 'THAT IS RIGHT' AND 'NO' 14

  PART 5– START WITH 'HOW' AND '
WHY' HELPS SOLVING PROBLEMS 16

  PART 6: – NON-VERBAL
COMMUNICATION..18

  PART 7– BARGAINING AND HAGGLING 20

  PART 8– BLACK SWAN' PROBLEM
AND THE PREPARATION................................22

ANALYSIS 24

QUIZ 26

QUIZ ANSWERS......................................32

CONCLUSION 33

INTRODUCTION

Never Split the Difference is a book written by Chris Voss and Tahl Raz. Voss works as a professor of negotiation at the University in Southern California Marshall School of Business and the Georgetown University McDonough School of Business, while Raz has already co-authored several books on leadership and business achievement together with Keith Ferrazzi and Gary Burnison. Raz also writes for many publications, including the *Wall Street Journal* and the *New York Times*.

Never Split the Difference is a book about negotiations. Negotiations take place in many different fields of life, such as business, and in some critical situations, like hostage situations. The book is actually a guide on how to best behave when certain things happen, regardless of whether that includes the need for negotiation techniques in hostage situations or in business. Throughout the book, the authors describe what to do, what kind of questions to ask, and how to react in a situation that requires negotiation. These techniques include active listening, assertive speech, knowing how to remain calm despite the situation, and many more.

Definitely a book that can teach its readers something new and useful, *Never Split the Difference* is a guide for both beginners and those who consider themselves to be experts at negotiation. It offers new perspectives that will help to improve anyone's negotiations skills.

SUMMARY

PART 1 – CONTROLLING THE EMOTIONS

The first part of the book is about human emotions. In this part, the authors write about how every good negotiator can gain an advantage in the negotiation process by controlling their emotions.

Many books and negotiation teachers say that when negotiating, people should be emotionless and highly logical. This means that during the negotiation process, people should entirely shutdown their emotions and that they should be lead entirely by their knowledge and logic. But when a negotiation is happening, this is hardly possible. The main reason for this is because almost every negotiation process, which includes some high-stake possibility and the outcome, will result in some kind of irrational behavior. Every good negotiator needs to know how to control his own emotions in order to achieve his goals. The authors describe how the book *Getting to Yes* is mostly written for professionals and is difficult for beginners to apply.

Why is it important to learn how to control emotions when negotiating?

As we wrote above, when emotions are not controlled, it can lead to irrational choices and decisions, which can have long-term consequences for both parties in the negotiation process. To prevent irrationality from happening, emotions need to be controlled and properly applied.

PART 2 –
ACTIVE LISTENING IS THE KEY

In the second part of the book, we read about active listening and how it can affect and greatly benefit both sides during a negotiation.

Why is active listening so important, especially when it comes to negotiations?

First of all, active listening makes the other side feel as though they are being listened to. When a negotiator is using active listening, the other person will see that their demands are acknowledged and respected. This will lead to a better and more successful negotiation.

What does the active listening look like?

An active listener speaks gently but with confidence. A person who actively listens to what another person is saying shows interest in what the other person is saying. This can be done by asking "sub-questions," focusing on the person when speaking to them, and maintaining eye contact. Maybe the most important part of active listening is maintaining dialogue. This can be done by asking questions (not in an interrogative manner but in calm and assertive way) about the subject. The opposite of this is a monologue where one person presents their rules and demands without giving the opportunity for other side to voice their opinions or conditions.

The authors also describe what active listeners do *not* look like. They do that by using examples from the movies *Speed* and *Die Hard*. In those examples, we can see that negotiator is shouting at the hostage taker. A negotiation should certainly not look like this. The negotiators in these movies not only yell at the hostage takers, but they also interrupt them, presenting their own demands and refusing to negotiate until the hostage takers agree to the negotiator's terms. It is clear that this type of negotiation will almost never have the desired outcome. That is why the authors describe active listening as an alternative.

A negotiator who is also an active listener will know how to resolve the situation and how to find a peaceful resolution to a standoff. This will also be the main goal of the active listening negotiator. His main goal is to resolve the situation in a peaceful way, while at the same time learning and understanding what the real motives of the other side are.

PART 3–
PRACTICE EMPATHY

This part is about empathy and why it is of crucial importance for every good negotiator.

By being empathetic we learn how the other side feels during the negotiation process. Also, if we are empathetic, we can also learn to recognize every potential hidden message and hidden meaning of the behavior of the other side.

That is why empathy is the ability to know how someone feels. However, empathy does not mean that we automatically agree with everything that the other side says or that we need to feel how the other side feels. A good negotiator, who is also empathetic, will know how the other side feels and why they feel the way they feel. This will improve the negotiator's chances in the negotiation process. When a negotiator acknowledges and states how the other person feels it is called labeling. Labeling is very useful and beneficial in the negotiation process because it increases trust between the two sides and removes the feeling that the other side failed to understand their feelings.

But although empathy is a trait that needs to be learned and practiced, sympathy is something that every good negotiator should be careful of.

Empathy means that a person understands how the other person feels. Because of that, a negotiator will know how to react and how to behave because they are getting a better picture of why the other side is asking for certain demands. The empathetic negotiator still maintains their position in the negotiation process. Even though the negotiator knows how the other person feels, they will still keep their original position in the negotiation process. Things will change if a negotiator starts experiencing sympathy for the other side, because this could cause a negotiator to change their terms. That could be very unpleasant, especially for those who are represented by the negotiator.

Connected with sympathy is the well-known "Stockholm syndrome."

Stockholm syndrome occurs when a person develops a close relationship with a kidnapper. Because of that, a person will do almost anything and everything the kidnapper tells them to do, because that person got too close to the kidnapper. But the real truth is that the person will cooperate with the kidnapper not because they really love or like them, but because of their own unconscious desire for self-preservation and survival.

When it comes to business, sympathy is also not desirable. If one side becomes sympathetic towards the other, the other side could exploit and use that sympathy in the future for their benefit, often damaging the other side.

PART 4: –
'THAT IS RIGHT' AND 'NO'

This chapter of the books speaks about which is the best way to manipulate the other side to agree to terms and solutions made by the other side. The best way to manipulate the other side to agree with the offered solution is to repeat everything that the other side has said, and then to say, "that is right."

By saying "that is right" or by showing any other sign of agreement, the negotiator shows that they "agree" with what the other side wants and says.

The word "no" can also be a very powerful tool when trying to reach certain points in a negotiation. Many negotiation specialists suggest that to successfully negotiate, one should use a series of questions, to which every answer has to be the affirmative "yes." However, the authors say that the word "no" has its own strength. By immediately saying "no" during a negotiation, two sides can also immediately identify the area of disagreement between them. Also, saying "yes" does not necessarily mean that the side will agree with what the other side suggested. Moreover, "yes" can be an "official" response to the question asked, even though the real answer is still hidden.

A typical example of this is when two or more parties agree on lowering carbon emissions in the atmosphere or decreasing their nuclear programs. All the sides can say "yes," but we are perfectly aware that that "yes" almost always means "no." If these parties are later confronted about it, they can say in their defense that they "wanted to decrease the emission of carbon dioxide into the atmosphere, but due to economic reasons that was impossible to achieve."

By starting a question with words such as "how" or "why," we can determine whether or not a goal is achievable. For instance, with divorced couples, one side can ask a question beginning with "how" to determine whether something will fit into the other's plans.

By starting our questions with either of these two question words, we can easily find out if the goal that we want to achieve is even possible to achieve, and how that goal fits into our "big picture."

PART 5– START WITH 'HOW' AND 'WHY' HELPS SOLVING PROBLEMS

In this chapter, the authors continue with the importance of the question words "how" and "why," suggesting that these question words should be used more often, especially when trying to negotiate. When asking questions that start with these words, we also invite the other party into the problem. That way it is more likely for both sides to cooperate in the negotiation, because both sides will use arguments which will lead to a solution.

But question words like "how" and "why" do not always help to solve a problem. There are situations where questions with these words can cause even more problems. There is an example of a young potential employee, who is trying to get a job in a respectable company. During a job interview, he might be asked a questions like "how long does he expect to work for us." This question can provoke a person, and in some people, especially if they are inexperienced, it can lead to irrational responses fueled by emotions and fear. This will happen almost every time a person is challenged if the comfort zone of that person is in danger of being compromised.

PART 6: –
NON-VERBAL COMMUNICATION

There are two ways that humans communicate: verbally and non-verbally. Even though many people believe that most communication takes place when we say words to one another, this is not exactly true. Most communication between people is non-verbal. This means that gestures, tone of voice, mimicry, and the rest of body language are actually the most important part of how people communicate. The same is true when negotiating.

It is believed that verbal communication makes up only seven percent of communication total. This means that the other ninety three percent of communication goes through body language, tone of voice and other non-verbal methods.

Many people pay little or no attention when it comes to non-verbal signs of communication. This happens mostly because of lack of knowledge. With knowledge, which tells us about the importance of non-verbal communication, we will greatly increase our chances for success in negotiations.

But one should be careful when examining non-verbal signs of communication. When searching for non-verbal signs, we should search for something that will show us that a person is behaving strangely or out of the ordinary. If and when we notice such uncommon behavior, before we react, we should ask that person about subjects that interests us rather than making pre-determined judgments, which are based on assumptions of our observations.

There are situations where we can be tricked by what non-verbal signs seem to tell us about certain people or situations. For instance, upon asking a question, a person can show a certain body reaction, which can tell us that there is a possibility that what that person is telling us is not true. But if we knew that person better, we would know that the person is not lying and that these are actually signs of anxiety, because they get anxious whenever they are in a social situation.

Non-verbal signs of communication are very helpful and thus it is good to know how to recognize them. Yet they can also lead to confusion. To avoid further confusion, the best thing to do is simply to ask about anything that is unclear to us.

PART 7–
BARGAINING AND HAGGLING

According to the authors, there are three types of bargaining styles: assertive, analytical and accommodating. Each style depends on how the negotiator intends to lead the negotiation process. But also each style of negotiation can be more successful if the negotiator uses progressive offers, which will make the other side believe that they are getting the most and the best possible.

Assertive and analytical negotiators are contradictory to one another. The assertive negotiator does not like to waste time, and thus speaks as quickly as possible. The analytical negotiator loves to use as much time as possible and pays attention to every aspect of the negotiation process, and then uses the information gained during the negotiation process.

Accommodative negotiators tend to speak in a friendly manner and often talk about things unrelated to the negotiation process. Their main goal is to ensure a positive and friendly relationship with the other side. It is good to recognize and be able to differentiate between these three types of negotiators because every type of negotiator is best for a certain type of negotiation. Sometimes assertive negotiators will be the best to use, while at other times an accommodator will be the best. An assertive negotiator's best use is often when bargaining or haggling, because these often require speed and swiftness. At other times, bargaining requires more time and a different strategy; this is when an accommodator is best.

PART 8– BLACK SWAN' PROBLEM AND THE PREPARATION

Here the authors speak about something that they call the "Black Swans." A Black Swan is something that can completely change the flow of the negotiation process.

It can literally be anything, from religious beliefs to market trends, which were unfamiliar when the negotiation started. When a Black Swan is uncovered, it can greatly impact and very often change how the negotiation process goes. A Black Swan always includes whatever things are currently the most important. That can be a person's life, money, health or well-being; it can be anything and it can significantly influence how the negotiation proceeds.

After this, the authors discuss what every successful negotiator needs to have. They say that every good negotiator has to possess enough knowledge about the situation in which he is about to negotiate and the other side participating in the negotiation. This is what the authors call "good preparation," and it also includes "one sheet." This one sheet is actually a piece of paper, which will contain the best and the worst case scenarios for the upcoming negotiation, a summary of the situation, emotions that could be labeled, potential accusations to look for, and calibrated questions to gain information about.

Good preparation for negotiation is very similar to good preparation for an upcoming exam. If prepared, there is a great chance of succeeding in passing that exam. If not prepared or if not prepared well enough, chances for success become much lower. The same goes for negotiations. If a negotiator is well prepared, his chances for success and for getting his terms become much higher. But, if a negotiator is not prepared well enough, then success becomes almost impossible to achieve.

The summary ends here.

ANALYSIS

Never Split the Difference was written in a "lecture style." It is narrated by entirely by Voss, rather than Raz, and this can particularly be seen when we look at the way the author explains everything. He presents his information as if he is lecturing his students and he does it in a very confident manner.

When analyzing chapters one by one, we see that each chapter begins with a hostage situation. Later in every chapter, the author gives explanations on how to solve the particular situation the best way possible. Every one of his solutions is based on Voss's lectures. Throughout the book, we can see that everything that both authors tried to tell the readers is said in easy-to-understand English. This means that the book is written for a wide audience and not just for those who are proficient in law terminology and negotiations. There are a few terms that may not be very accessible to the average reader, but their appearance is minimal.

Chris Voss is an expert in negotiation and hostage situations and has even worked for the FBI. Together with Tahl Raz, he has managed to write a book that tells us what the best course of action is when a situation demands quick thinking and thinking ahead. These traits are always almost needed during negotiations, whether in business or hostage situations.

QUIZ

For all readers who like the book and want to put their knowledge to the test, this quiz is what they need. Questions are easy to answer and every answer can be found within 'summary' and 'quiz answers' sections. So let's get started.

QUESTION 1

Why is saying 'no' almost always good when it comes to negotiation?

    a) By saying 'no' we immediately show who is 'in charge' of the entire situation.

    b) When both sides say 'no' they show that they share disagreements in similar areas of negotiation.

    c) Saying 'no' is necessary because by giving affirmative answers to every demand will show that we are can be manipulated.

    d) Everything above.

QUESTION 2

New information, something that can greatly impact the 'flow' of negotiation process, something that was not known before is called...

a) ...Black Frog.

b) ...Black Fish.

c) ...Black Swan.

d) ...Black Stork.

QUESTION 3

"Assertive and analytical negotiators are contradictory to one another."

TRUE   FALSE

QUESTION 4

"_____negotiators tend to speak in friendly manner and when they speak they often speak about certain things, which are unconnected to _____.
Their main goal is to ensure _____ and _____ relationship with the other side."

QUESTION 5

Why is beneficial for every good negotiator to practice empathy?

    a) Because empathy shows us that we care for other side.

    b) By being empathetic we are able to see how other side feels and thus react accordingly.

    c) By being empathetic we can feel how other side feels but remain at the 'same side' where we are.

    d) Everything above.

QUESTION 6

"When we actively listen to someone, that someone will see that their demands are acknowledged and respected."

TRUE   FALSE

QUESTION 7

Why is sympathy a 'bad' and undesirable when it comes to negotiations?

- a) Sympathetic person tend to go to the 'other side' and thus they forget the conditions they represent.

- b) When feeling sympathy we will usually try to understand how other person feels and we will try to 'ease' our demands.

- c) 'a' and 'b'.

- d) None of the above.

QUESTION 8

"If _____ is well prepared (or prepared the best way possible) his chances for success and for _____ his _____ become much higher and more likely possible to happen. But, if _____ is not prepared well enough and/or if he is not prepared at all then the chances for _____ become almost impossible to achieve."

QUESTION 9

It is believed that verbal part of communication takes how many percent of the communication altogether?

   a) 15

   b) 2

   c) 6

   d) 7

QUESTION 10

When it comes to negotiation what is contrary to, what the author calls as the 'active listening'?

a) 'Passive listening.'

b) Monologue.

c) Aggressive demands.

d) Everything above.

QUESTION 11

"To prevent irrationality from happening, emotions need to be controlled and properly 'applied'."

TRUE   FALSE

QUIZ ANSWERS

QUESTION 1 – b

QUESTION 2 – c

QUESTION 3 – TRUE

QUESTION 4 – "accommodative, the negotiation process, positive, friendly."

QUESTION 5 – c

QUESTION 6 – TRUE

QUESTION 7 – c

QUESTION 8 – "a negotiator, negotiating, terms, a negotiator, success."

QUESTION 9 – d

QUESTION 10 – b

QUESTION 11 – TRUE

CONCLUSION

For every reader who wanted a book about negotiation and how to lead a negotiation with the maximum chance for success, *Never Split the Difference* is just the right read. It is a book written by Chris Voss, an expert in negotiations, together with Tahl Raz, a writer for the *New York Journal*.

Reading this book is like reading top secret confidential documents. It is filled with thrill and the reader never knows what they will find out by reading the next page. The thing I liked most about the book is how the author, although an expert in his field regarding negotiation, uses language that is easy to understand for every reader. Sure, there are certain parts of the book which contain some harder to understand terminology, but that is minimal. The book is written so that almost everyone who is interested in how to get the best when doing a negotiation will be able to understand.

Never Split the Difference is divided into several chapters. In every part of the book, Voss explains a certain aspect of the negotiation process. All the parts together form a perfect whole, which looks great, but readers do not necessarily need to read every single part to get a firm grasp on what the book is about. Every part has something that the previous parts did not have and every part opens a new window into the negotiation process.

And when it comes to a negotiation, there are many aspects and many things to learn. That is why Voss speaks of the importance of active listening to the other side, empathy (but not sympathy), the importance of saying "yes" and "no" at the right times, different types of negotiators, and something that he calls the "Black Swan." This is something that I liked a lot. The Black Swan can be anything that influences the course of the negotiation process – something that both sides did not know prior to the beginning of the negotiation, but when they find out, it will definitely impact the flow of negotiation or can even terminate it.

Educational, easy-to-read, written in professional manner, but with a minimal use of complicated terminology, *Never Split the Difference* is a book that every good negotiator or any person who want to be a good negotiator should definitely read. It contains many facts and things that many of us probably did not know, but that can greatly influence how our negotiations proceed in the future.

I definitely recommend reading this book. Many readers will find it so interesting and educational that they will want to read it a second time. *Never Split the Difference* is a book for both professional and everyday use.

Thank You, and more...

Thank you for spending your time to read this book, I hope now you hold a greater knowledge about **Never Split the Difference.**

There are like-minded individuals like you who would like to learn about **Never Split the Difference,** this information can be useful for them as well. So, I would highly appreciate if you post a good review on amazon kindle where you purchased this book. And to share it in your social media (Facebook, Instagram, etc.)

Not only does it help me make a living, but it helps others obtain this knowledge as well. So I would highly appreciate it!!

www.amazon.com

FURTHER READINGS

If you are interested in other book summaries, feel free to check out the summaries below.

1. Summary – Mindset: The New Psychology of Success
   https://www.amazon.com/dp/B078MV4S93/

2. Summary – Good to Great
   https://www.amazon.com//dp/B078H4CMB9/

3. Summary – The Nightingale
   https://www.amazon.com/dp/B078RV7XQQ/

4. Summary – StrengthsFinder 2.0
   https://www.amazon.com/dp/B078R4N79W/

5. Summary – Getting Things Done
   https://www.amazon.com//dp/B078YPTN8S/

   To find other book summaries, click the link below:
   https://www.amazon.com/s/ref=nb_sb_noss?url=search-alias%3Daps&field-keywords=fastdigest+summary

Made in the USA
Lexington, KY
26 January 2019